WHAT?!

WHAT?!

The **Wisdom**, **Heart**, **Attitude**, & **Tenacity** of a Godly Woman

DORIS W. SANDERS

KEEN VISION PUBLISHING

Printed in the United States of America
Keen Vision Publishing, LLC
www.keen-vision.com
ISBN: 978-1-948270-73-1

In Loving Memory of my friend, lover, partner, and husband, Joel Sanders, Sr. You are forever in my heart.

TABLE OF CONTENTS

Introduction   9

Chapter One What Did You Say To Me?   13

Chapter Two Girl, You Better WISE Up!   31

Chapter Three You Can't Give Up!   45

Chapter Four The Heart of the Matter   59

Chapter Five Be Transformed   73

Chapter Six Endure the Pruning   83

Words From the Author   95

Acknowledgments   99

About the Author   105

A Message to the World   107

Stay Connected   109

INTRODUCTION

WHAT?! was once my response whenever someone tried to give me wisdom or advice. It's amazing how God has used this response to title my first book: WHAT?!: The Wisdom, Heart, Attitude, and Tenacity of a Godly Woman. You see, I haven't always been a woman who could share Godly wisdom with others. The heart that now loves others freely was once sick with anger, bitterness, disappointment, and frustration. My attitude was "tore up from the floor up," and I was tenacious about the wrong things ... BUT GOD!

This book is more than a testimony of how God has transformed me. It is filled with the wisdom, strength, and instruction I gained along the way. My prayer is that as you read this book, you will be encouraged to allow God to transform your entire life and give you a testimony to share with the world. Within the pages of this book, I share my story of how God walked me through every curveball the enemy threw my way. I transparently share how I overcame singleness, grief, multiple marriages, relationships, sickness, and the process of healing, all while doing the best I could to raise my four exceptional children. I will share the truth about my situations and what God taught me about me every step of the way.

My journey has been far from perfect, but each time I fell short of God's glory, He was there to pick me up and get me back on track. Each time, He reminded me that the story I had to tell would transform the lives of all who read it. At the time, I assumed God just wanted me to talk about my life with those I encountered. Never did I imagine His desire was for me to become an author.

It took me three years to complete this book. The closer I got to finishing it, the more God would tell me to write. On the days when I didn't want to work on my book, God would speak and say, "Doris, someone is waiting on your story." There were times when I didn't think it would matter if I got this book done or not. However, when I look back over all I've endured, when I see the hand of God in every situation of my life, and when I realize that I am only here today by the goodness and grace of God, I realize that this story is too good to keep to myself!

More than anything, as you read this book, I want you to know that there is HOPE! Your situation is not too bad, and you are not too messed up for God. If He can take my mess and turn it into a message, I know He can and will do the same thing for you.

At the end of each chapter, you will find space for you to write your top three takeaways from each chapter, as well as a prayer and an assignment. You can complete everything in the book, or you can write it in your journal. I want to encourage you to do more than read this book. Be an active learner! Allow the wisdom in this book to open your eyes and transform you into the woman God always desired you to be.

Are you ready to talk about the true wisdom, heart, attitude, and tenacity of a Godly woman? If so, I'll meet you in Chapter One!

Do all things without grumbling or questioning, that you may be blameless and innocent, children of God without blemish in the midst of a crooked and twisted generation, among whom you shine as lights in the world.

Philippians 2:14-15 (ESV)

CHAPTER ONE

WHAT DID YOU SAY TO ME?

Back in the late 80s, I was the type of woman who never stepped a toe outside unless my hair was laid, and my makeup was in place. I also took great pride in what I wore. My shoes had to match my bag, and I loved wearing nice suits to work. It felt good to look great, but I also loved the attention my appearance drew from others. Women envied me because their boyfriends (and sometimes husbands) couldn't take their eyes off me. I was all of that and a bag of chips. This was before I had children, so I had a lovely shape, flawless skin, and long natural hair and nails. Honestly, the makeup and extra things I did only enhanced my physical traits. I didn't need it, but

I wouldn't be caught dead without it.

At the time, I lived in Atlanta, GA, and worked at a local phone company. One day, the company experienced a major computer crash, and our work schedule became hectic, to say the least. You see, back in the '80s, technology wasn't as advanced as it is now. We had to unbox documents that had been prepared to be shipped to our vendors and users and spend crazy hours rekeying lost information back into the computers. We were at work so much, we only had time to run home, take a nap, freshen up, and return to work. This meant no time for makeup, hair, nails, suits, heels, or matching purses. Everyone dressed like they were going to the gym.... including me. I hated every minute of it. I had a little peace about it because everyone looked their absolute worse.

As though it were yesterday, I remember when my coworkers and I got the great news that we were caught up and would resume regular office hours the following Monday. We were so excited that we exited the building like a rushing wind. I walked out of the building looking a hot mess, and couldn't wait to go to the drug store and buy some makeup to look my best on Monday. I lived on the Southside of Atlanta, so it was more convenient for me to use public transportation, the MARTA.

As I stood at the bus stop thinking about cleaning my house, getting some rest, and putting myself together again, a gentleman I worked with approached me.

"Can I give you a ride home?" he asked.

"No," I replied very sharply.

"May I ask why not?"

"I have some errands to run."

He was very persistent and refused to accept no for an answer. "Where do you have to go?" he asked kindly.

Now don't get me wrong, ladies. The man was fine. He was dark-skinned, tall, in great shape, and bow-legged. I was so short with him because I looked a mess. I prayed the bus would come before he got a good look at me.

"I'm going to the drug store," I replied.

"For medication?" he asked.

"No. Make-up," I responded. I was starting to get very uncomfortable. I thought to myself, surely this man will look at me closely and stop talking to me, but his response took me by surprise.

"You are beautiful," he said. "You don't need to wear any makeup."

I looked at him and finally decided to take him up on his offer. I jumped in his car and wore a smile all the way home. When we arrived at my apartment, I prayed he wouldn't ask to come in because my apartment was a mess.

"I would invite you in, but my place is in a mess," I told him.

"I can come in and help you clean your place, and afterward, we can go and clean mine," he said with a smile.

I had to turn that offer down because I didn't want him to come inside my apartment. When he left, I began to clean up my place. The first place I attacked was my bathroom. No, not the tub or the toilet, but my counter. I threw away the foundation, face powder, eye shadow, eyeliner, blush, and every container of makeup I owned. Why? Because I realized that the makeup didn't make me beautiful. I finally looked in the mirror and realized that I was a beautiful woman without it.

Later that week, we went out for lunch, and it was amazing. I didn't lack male attention before him. Honestly, because of my looks, I was accustomed to getting whatever I wanted from any man. However, very few of them were interested in me because of my heart. There were plenty of times I got what I wanted just because of how I looked. It felt so refreshing to have someone accept the natural me, instead of the made-up version. One thing led to another, and we began to see each other a lot more. I learned that this man was just as beautiful inside as he was outside. He was kind, funny, sweet, intelligent, and very caring.

I was born and raised in the country, so if there

was one thing I knew how to do well, it was taking care of a man. There was nothing I wouldn't and didn't do for him. My mindset was, "Whatever my man likes, I'm going to give it to him so that no other woman has the opportunity to give it to him." I have always had a passion for cooking and baking, so I always ensured he was fed well. One of our favorite desserts was red velvet cake. One day, I decided to make one for him. He enjoyed it a lot more than I did. For some reason, the sight, smell, and taste of that red velvet cake made me sick to my stomach. I would vomit just thinking about it.

I brushed this off and just assumed I had a stomach virus.

A month later, one of my coworkers and close friends encouraged me to go to the doctor. I took her advice and found out that it wasn't a stomach virus. I was pregnant.

This news couldn't have come at a worse time. I thought I was living the best of my life. I was fine, living it up with my new man, and had a bank account that overflowed. I knew that being pregnant meant that my nice body would soon transform. I wouldn't be able to be as free as I had been, and the money I had would have to be spent differently. On top of that, I had to share the news with my man. I was scared, but I didn't dare let it come across to him. I didn't know what he was going to say, and by the time I dialed his number to tell him, I didn't care.

As soon as he picked up the phone, I raged full speed ahead like a wild bull.

"We need to talk!" I said with an attitude.

"What? You call yourself pregnant?" he guessed correctly.

"I don't call myself pregnant. I am pregnant! You're the daddy, and I don't want to hear any of that crazy stuff you have to say!" I snapped.

Naturally, he reacted right back to my nasty attitude.

A couple of months later, I realized that I could have handled the situation differently, but I didn't care to go back and fix it. My pride wouldn't let me. I told myself that it didn't matter how I said it; he should have been nicer to me.

Throughout my pregnancy, I constantly reminded him that we didn't need his money or his presence. I tried proving this repeatedly to myself, but at the end of the day, my heart was heavy with the pain of loneliness and unforgiveness. I was too selfish to ask him over or accompany me to any doctor's appointments.

I would often sit and wonder how he and I got to this point. Everything started perfectly. I couldn't understand why we had parted ways after a few months of dating. The truth is, in addition to seeing my natural beauty, this man could also recognize

WHAT DID YOU SAY TO ME?

the condition of my heart. Even though I did all the right things as it relates to being fun, available, and showing that I cared, my attitude soon caused us to part ways. My nasty attitude led to me being a single mother. Don't get me wrong; I'm not making any excuses for him leaving me to parent my firstborn child alone. However, looking back on it, I can see how my attitude made it difficult for him to be in our lives. Becoming a single mother was a major wake-up call for me. It opened my eyes to the fact that my life was not based on how beautiful I was, but how smart and healed I was.

My infatuation with my looks didn't start when I became an adult. As a child, I was always told how beautiful and pretty I was. Needless to say, as I grew up, this went to my head. I learned early on that my looks would get me whatever I wanted without me working for it. So I grew to depend on my looks and made sure I always presented myself well. When I became a mother, I realized that I had to let go of the high-maintenance habits, because I was responsible for another life. Without my high-maintenance attire, I realized that I lacked a lot of substance.

During my pregnancy, there were plenty of days and nights that I couldn't do anything but cry. My pride would not allow me to tell others that I needed help and couldn't do it along. I kept my child's father in the dark as much as I could. I only communicated with him on Sundays. Whenever we talked, I wanted to ask him to change his mind and be apart of our lives, but I couldn't find the words. I didn't know what to say, and I was too proud to communicate that.

A man shouldn't cause you to change. However, if we look at every relationship, connection, and encounter we have with others from the right angle, we can learn a lesson or two about ourselves.

I was raised in church, so even once I moved to Atlanta, I kept that routine. Even though I attended services weekly, I only sought to get high off emotions instead of allowing Holy Spirit to work in me. When I would listen to the sermons, I would only listen for things that proved I was right in my thinking. I ignored anything that didn't make me feel good about myself. Since I assumed I had it all together and didn't need God's help, God left me to my prideful thinking. It was almost as if God said, "Okay, I'm going to let you do things your way so you can see how far you will make it without me." It didn't take long for me to realize I wouldn't get too far.

After I had my daughter, I went back to work with my head held high, dressed to the nines. By this point, everyone knew who my child's father was and that we were no longer together. We all worked together, so everyone knew the situation. I knew I had to keep a good face even though I was sad, confused, and frustrated on the inside. I didn't want anyone to think I was down and out, even though I was. I never missed a beat, and my attitude was still jacked up.

My daughter's father and I would see each other two to three times a week and walk right past each other as if we were strangers. I was determined to be a strong, black, independent woman. So despite how often I felt like I needed to say something, I never did. One day, I decided to give him a call at work. Of course, that didn't go over too well, because even though my loneliness drove me to call him, my negative attitude barely let the man get a word in. I was quick to remind him that we didn't need him. That drove him further away. Again, I'm not making any excuses for him not being in my daughter's life. However, as I look back on those times, I realize how I made it hard for him to be there. I made myself so unapproachable. I wanted to prove to him and others that I didn't need a man to take care of my child.

One day, I was home alone with my daughter. She was crying uncontrollably. I was tired, thinking about how I would make ends meet, and I became overwhelmed. I found myself on my face crying and calling out to God for guidance. The reality of being a single mother humbled me and brought me to my knees. I realized more than ever that if I was going to make it, I had to learn how to depend on God and allow Him to fix the ugly areas within me. The first area we had to work on was my attitude, especially my pride. As God began to show me how ugly my pride made me and how it was hindering me from getting the support I needed with my daughter, I surrendered. I cried out and told God that I needed help. He brought people into my life who were willing to support and love both my daughter and me.

When my daughter turned thirteen, she met her dad for the first time. After years of not communicating, he and I also spoke for the first time. He took the lead and apologized for his actions and thanked me for taking such good care of our daughter. During this conversation, he expressed how even though he knew I was a good woman, my negative attitude overpowered everything else. As I think back on this conversation, I regret that I didn't know the detriment of a negative attitude. My pridefulness and snappy ways not only impacted my life but my daughter's life as well. There was once a time when I hated to reflect on that relationship with my daughter's father. However, today, I am grateful for that relationship. It gave me three of the greatest gifts anyone could ever give me. 1. It taught me how to see my natural beauty. 2. It made me realize that I had spent so much time working on my outer appearance that I didn't think about the inner me. And finally, and most importantly, that relationship gave me my firstborn child.

Ladies, there is absolutely nothing wrong with wanting to look good and be attractive. However, your good looks won't amount to much if your attitude is ugly. The word attitude is defined as, a settled way of thinking or feeling about someone or something, typically reflected in a person's behavior. Everyone has an attitude. Having an attitude about something isn't bad. We are supposed to have an attitude. However, we must ensure that we possess a Godly attitude rather than a negative attitude. When we possess a Godly attitude, we exude love, grace, and patience to those around us. Just as the definition says, our attitudes are reflected in our behavior. Our attitudes are internal, and to look good on the outside, we must first look good on the inside. If you have a bad attitude, you don't even have to say anything for people to recognize it. They can see it in your countenance, how you walk, and even how you hold your body. To appear more welcoming, you must first do the internal work and allow God to fix your attitude.

Many of you reading this book may feel like there is nothing wrong with your negative attitude. You may not even feel like your attitude is negative. You may feel like you are entitled to feel how you feel and say what you want to say; however you want to say it. While you have the freedom to do just that, understand that it will be detrimental to your life, success, and dreams.

Did you know that your attitude can be the reason

why you can't make friends, get the job you want, or even get married? You can be the most beautiful woman in the world, but eventually, people will get tired of looking at you. You must have substance, and most importantly, you must have a positive and Godly attitude.

A GODLY ATTITUDE

Having a Godly attitude doesn't mean that everything will be perfect in your life, or that you won't have days and moments when you are angry, upset, mad, or frustrated. On the contrary, having a Godly attitude is all about how you act and respond when you have those rough moments. Having a Godly attitude doesn't mean you won't disagree with others, dislike certain things, or be disappointed. Having a Godly attitude changes how you communicate how you feel. When you possess a Godly attitude, you look at difficult situations differently. Instead of acting on your anger, you choose to pray about it. Instead of cursing people out, you take your frustrations to God. Instead of being rude, you communicate how you feel with respect. Possessing a Godly attitude changes how we see and respond to those around us. It is necessary if we are going to become everything God has called us to be.

So, how do we go about possessing a Godly attitude? I'm glad you asked. First, you must seek God.

The Bible tells us that while man looks at the outer appearance, God looks at the heart. So, even though the world may see us and think that we are amazing, God can look at our hearts and see the ugly things that no one else can see. He can see what we haven't realized, and He can see the things that we choose to ignore. When you seek God, you must be bold enough to ask Him to reveal the ugly parts of you to you. This is not an easy process, so you will need to also ask Him to give you the strength to face the truth about yourself.

After you ask God to reveal the ugly parts, surrender and submit yourself to His process to heal you. You see, for many of us, our negative attitudes are just the residue of the pain we have endured. It's possible that you are not mad at the world; you are just mean because you had to be tough to survive. It's possible that you don't mean to be so negative, but because life has disappointed you so much, you don't know how to be hopeful. You really don't want to be rude to other people, but you've just been hurt so many times that you no longer know how to trust others. Beyond that snappy attitude and frowning face is a lot of hurt and pain. If you want to have a Godly attitude, you must allow God to heal those places within you.

As you allow God in and surrender to His process, keep in mind that things won't be fixed immediately.

It will take some time to work through your issues, and that's okay. You may even have days where you go back to the old you. When you do slip, make sure you go back to God and repent. Know that it doesn't matter how bad you have messed up; God is still standing with open arms ready to get you back on track. Give everything over to Him and allow Him to change you. Don't give up on yourself or your process.

This process of adjusting your attitude may be difficult, but it is worth it, girlfriend. Aren't you ready to be as beautiful inside as you are outside? Let's Pray!

Heavenly Father,

Thank you for being willing to work with us through our imperfections. Thank you for being a Father who loves us despite our flaws. We confess that there are areas in our lives that we need to work on, especially our attitudes. We ask that you would search our hearts. If there is anything in our hearts that is not like you, we ask that you reveal it. Show us the root of this issue and heal us in this area. God, we want to be loving, kind, and patient with those around us. We want to look and sound like you. When people encounter us, we want them to encounter you. To do that, we must possess a God-ly attitude. Give us the strength to endure your process of perfecting us. In Jesus' name we pray, Amen.

ACTIVITY ONE

This assignment may be difficult, but I want you to do it. Pray and ask God to highlight one person you can trust to be honest with you. When God reveals that person to you, ask them to answer the following questions about you. Be sure to write their responses in the space provided. This activity will help you understand how you come across to others. It will reveal the areas that you may be overlooking. No matter what the person says, be sure to have an open heart. Don't be upset with them if they reveal something that hurts. Thank them for their honesty, pray about it, and allow God to heal those areas within you.

How would you describe my attitude?

Are there times when I am stubborn, rude, mean, or snappy?

How do I respond to hard situations?

What are three areas I need to work on?

TAKE 3!

In the space below, write your top three take-aways from this chapter.

Blessed is the one who finds wisdom, and the one who gets understanding, for the gain from her is better than gain from silver and her profit better than gold. She is more precious than jewels, and nothing you desire can compare with her. Long life is in her right hand; in her left hand are riches and honor. Her ways are ways of pleasantness, and all her paths are peace....

Proverbs 3:13-18 (ESV)

CHAPTER TWO

GIRL, YOU BETTER WISE UP!

Even though she grew up without her biological father, my daughter, Jessica, turned out just fine. God has a way of working things out despite how we make a mess of them. One of the many things she does now is preach. Twenty-six years after the ordeal with her father, my daughter taught a sermon that I will never forget. It was called, "How to Listen to God." She delivered this message from Joshua 1:1-11. In her message, she gave three instructions for hearing God properly: 1. Shut-Up 2. Listen-up 3. Read the word of God.

As she delivered this message, I sat and listened. It touched me at my core, and I wished I had heard this message a lot sooner. At one point in my life, I didn't shut-up because I thought I was always right. I didn't listen-up because I felt what I had to say was more important than what everyone else said. And I certainly didn't read God's word. As a result, I didn't possess the wisdom I needed to handle many situations correctly. I was very selfish and thought I had it all figured out. Life, of course, soon proved me wrong.

Have you ever read the Bible story found in John 4 about the Samaritan Woman? If not, take a look. That woman was me. Even before I met my daughter's father, I sought love and attention from other men, even those who were not mine. I was not concerned about who I hurt, as long as I was satisfied. For that reason, many of the lessons I've learned throughout my life happened in my many relationships. I honestly believe God knew that was the only way He could get me to understand the changes I needed to make in my life. In this chapter, I will teach you about the importance of being a woman who has Godly wisdom. Allow me to tell you about one of the many instances in my life that caused me to learn and value wisdom.

As I said in the previous chapter, most of my young adult years were spent in Atlanta. In addition to having a snappy attitude, I was a fighter. I put my hands on just about every man I dated. You see, growing up, I often witnessed my mother being abused by men.

When I got older, I was determined to get them be-fore they got me. I refused to allow any man to put his hands on me and get away with it. I learned how to use my hands before I learned to use my mouth.

Before I met my firstborn's father, for two years, I dated a man. We practically lived together. Despite how much we enjoyed spending time with each oth-er, we were always fussing and fighting about some-thing. One Sunday evening, I was sitting in my bath-room, rolling my hair. It was a nice peaceful evening. My guy walked in the bathroom, said something to me, and walked out. I wasn't clear what he said, so I got up and walked behind him.

"What did you say?" I asked kindly.

He didn't respond. He just started hitting me. Before I knew it, my head was going from side to side, and hair rollers were flying everywhere. My face burned, and it felt like my eyeballs were falling out of my head.

After he put a beating on me, I sat there in disbe-lief. I couldn't believe he had gotten the best of me. After he was done, we walked out the door.

I called my sister and told her what happened. Since I lived with the guy, she told me she was com-ing to pick me up. She said, "When I get downstairs, I am going to blow my horn one time. If you don't come down those stairs, I am going to come up there shooting!"

I thank God I heard the first horn. I went to stay with my sister for four days. My face and eyes were so bruised I had to wake up 30 minutes early to let my eyes adjust to the sunlight. I continued to go to work, and sometimes I would wear shades to hide the bruises and my pain. I didn't talk to the guy during these days. He would even call me on my job, and I wouldn't answer the phone.

I didn't take anything with me when I left, so I bought new clothes every day. Well, my mind started to think about all the nice clothes I had left behind and how I was going to get them back. One Friday, while I was at work, I called him and told him I was coming back home. He was so excited and started to apologize and tell me how much he loved me. Little did he know, but I wasn't coming back to stay. When he picked me up at the train station that night, he greeted me with a hug and kiss. On our way home, we stopped and got something to eat. When we got home, we slept together, and I would be lying if I said I didn't enjoy it. As I laid in his arms, all I could think about was how he had beaten me. I kept my eyes on him to make sure he didn't make any sudden moves, but I played right along with him and acted like everything was okay.

The next morning, I wasted no time. I got out of bed and started packing my things. He asked what I was doing, and I told him I was doing some spring cleaning. When he left to take his youngest brother to a softball game, I began to move quickly. I called my cousin and told him to come and move me. Shortly after, my cousin pulled up with a truck, and we began loading my stuff to move it to the other side of town. We had to make about two trips to get all of my things.

As we were loading up the last of my things, the guy pulled up and asked what I was doing. I didn't say anything. The guy got upset, but I was with my cousin, and he wasn't having it. He had no choice but to let me go.

Shortly after this relationship, I got into another bad relationship. I ended up having to decide at 2:00 a.m. to escape and find a way to move back to Alabama with my mother and stepdad. Even though I loved living in Atlanta, it presented me with too many opportunities to fall into temptations. I had a lot of healing to do, and I wasn't rooted in God enough to remain there.

I found myself in abusive relationships because I was always so ready to fight men. I didn't realize that I couldn't just go around putting my hands on people because I was angry. Anyone would get tired of that, and a few of the men did. Something inside of me fought men because I'd watched my mother be abused so much. It was as if I retaliated against men because I couldn't fight off the men who abused my mother. I had so much anger built up inside me, and I lacked the wisdom I needed to deal with it.

Once I moved back to Alabama, I began to reflect on many of the decisions I'd made with men. If I had Godly wisdom, I wouldn't have found myself in many of those situations. Wisdom is defined as the soundness of an action or decision with regard to the application of experience, knowledge, and good judgment. I made so many bad decisions about men because I lacked Godly wisdom. Very often, I did what made me feel good. Instead of seeking God for wisdom in my relationships, I allowed my brokenness, loneliness, and desire for a man to choose for me. As a result, I ended up in a lot of unhealthy relationships.

Lacking wisdom doesn't just impact our relationships. As I said before, this was just an area God used to teach me many lessons. Lacking wisdom can also impact our lives, careers, friendships, and even our relationship with God. The Bible says in James 1:5 (NLT), "If you need wisdom, ask our generous God, and he will give it to you. He will not rebuke you for asking."

Most of the time, when we have to make decisions, we do whatever we feel like doing instead of asking God for wisdom in making a decision. When we lean to our understanding, we end up in bad predicaments instead of the blessing God wanted us to have. James 1:5 lets us know that God is always there and available to give us guidance and instruction. Yes, God gave us free will, but He desires us to seek Him before we make decisions for our lives. This honors God and shows Him that we desire to be in His will.

I know, ladies. Sometimes, we think we know everything and have it all together. We don't want to come off as helpless or unsure. However, in our strive to be strong and independent women, we must depend on God. When we lean to God and seek His wisdom, life is a lot sweeter. It still won't be perfect, but we will know that we are in God's will and plan for our lives.

We can also obtain Godly wisdom from the wise counsel God places in our lives. Sometimes, God will send people into our lives to help us through difficult situations. We must allow these people to help us and give us advice. Many of the difficulties we face could have been avoided if we had only sought wisdom on the situation.

I want you to take a moment and think about every difficult situation you've ever been in. How could that situation had been different if you would have sought Godly wisdom?

We don't just need Godly wisdom for big decisions; we need it for everything we encounter throughout the day. When something goes wrong at work, before we react, we should stop and ask God for wisdom on how to handle the situation. Before we fuss at our children or pull out the belt, we should stop and ask for Godly wisdom to discipline them. I know buying nice things is fun, but we should seek God's wisdom even before we make purchases. It may seem like a lot to do, but we must seek Godly wisdom for every area in our lives!

The next time you are faced with choices, challenge yourself to stop, breathe, and assess the situation correctly. This can be anything from choosing a man to determining whether or not to take a trip. Before you make a decision, settle yourself and give yourself space to be quiet and hear God clearly. Next, pray about the choices you are faced with. Ask God to give you insight and wisdom. Finally, before you close your prayer, ask God to give you the strength to be obedient. Whatever God instructs you to do, act on it. Don't be afraid or disobedient.

If you take these steps when making decisions, you will notice how drastically your life changes. As you seek God for wisdom in all things, you will gain wisdom to share with those around you. Taking these steps gave me the wisdom to put in this book for women all over the world. Now, I am a published author! Seeking Godly wisdom certainly pays off. What will seeking Godly wisdom do for you? Let's Pray!

Mighty God,

We recognize you as being all-knowing and all-powerful. You know our end from our beginning. You have a plan and a purpose for our lives, and it is good. We come to you now, first asking for forgiveness for the many times we did not seek your wisdom or guidance for our lives. We apologize for being prideful enough to think that we know everything. Life has taught us that there is so much left for us to learn. God, we humble ourselves now and ask that you give us wisdom for every difficulty we face. Show us how to make decisions not just for right now, but for our future. Remind us to seek you in everything we do instead of leaning on our limited understanding. We love you, and thank you in advance. In Jesus' name we pray, Amen.

ACTIVITY TWO

In the space provided, write about a time in which you should have sought Godly wisdom, but you didn't. How did that situation turn out? What did that situation teach you? How will you handle things differently now?

WHAT?!

TAKE 3!

*In the space below, write your top three take-aways
from this chapter.*

And let us not grow weary of doing good, for in due season we will reap, if we do not give up.

Galatians 6:9 (ESV)

CHAPTER THREE

YOU CAN'T GIVE UP!

o you remember the last relationship I referenced at the end of Chapter Two? Well, it was a little more than just a relationship. I was married, and the marriage ended horribly. That was the straw that broke the camel's back, and I decided to move back to Alabama.

One of the best things I gained from that relationship was my one and only son, James. As a single mother with two children, I knew I had to work harder and provide for them. These two children brought so much joy to my life, and I didn't let anyone or anything get in the way of me providing for them.

When we still lived in Atlanta, I worked hard to

make sure they were taken care of. Unless I had to work or handle some important errands, my children were always with me. I didn't have a car, so we rode the MARTA everywhere we needed to go. Some days, we would have to be up by 4 am to make sure they got to school/daycare, and I got to work on time. It was tough, but I knew I had to do what was necessary for their wellbeing. Despite the heavy load of being a mother, I was never late for work. I was determined not to fail my children. They needed me, and I needed them.

A few years after we moved to Alabama, I remarried (we'll talk about this more later) and had my last two babies, my daughters, Joanna and Jermeka. The fight to be a good mother to my children got even more exciting. Now, I was not only a wife but also a mother to four amazing children. I made a promise to God, myself, and my children that they would never have to know the struggles I faced in life. I prayed harder, worked harder, and listened more. I fought for the life I knew my children deserved.

Many said that my husband and I were too strict on the kids, but it didn't matter to me. I wanted them to be better than we were. We didn't permit them to act like clowns or do many of the things other children around them did. We had high expectations for them and expected them to operate according to those standards.

I raised my children in church, and they were a part of every youth service at every church we attended. If we didn't know there would be a youth service before we got there, I still made sure they participated. I would pull out the Bible, and they would all read a Bible verse. People always complimented my children on how well they spoke in church. It made me proud.

When it came to academics, I didn't play. Each of my children will tell you that today. Sometimes, we laugh and joke about how hard I was on them academically, but they each will tell you they are grateful that I pushed them. I saw my children's bright futures, and I made sure that I did everything in my power to see them come to pass. I didn't want my children to miss their dreams because they didn't have what it took.

I didn't accept B's in my house. It was all A's or nothing. In my house, B stood for Beating. This might sound cruel, and I probably could have been a little more lenient, but I saw my children's potential. I didn't give room or space to slacking.

During summer breaks, my children only got to use one month of the summer for fun. The other months were spent learning, and I made it enjoyable. While other children were playing outside or watching TV, my children were learning reading, writing, math, science, and social studies. Every now and then, if they got done early, I would allow them to go outside to play.

Other children, even some of their relatives, teased my children and even called them book worms. I told them to keep their heads up, stay focused on their school work, and it would all pay off. Each year, they saw the fruit of their hard work. In May, before school dismissed for the summer, their school had an awards program where the students were award-ed for their hard work and labor. Every year, I would leave the Awards Program like I had went shopping. I would come home with all of their trophies, certifi-cates, awards, and medals. My husband and I would be so proud of them. Our children didn't just get awarded for their academic accomplishments; they also received awards for being good helpers, having great behavior, attendance, spelling bees, sports, etc. They were absolutely amazing students.

I can recall each of their dreams when they were younger. I remember hearing them say what they wanted to be when they grew up. Each time, I would pray to God for the strength to help them see their dreams come true. I can proudly say that each of them grew up to be what they dreamed and more. Jessica, the oldest, read more than any of my chil-dren. She could always be found with her nose in a book. She won every spelling bee she participated in and always scored the highest in the Accelerated Readers program. She always wanted to be a teacher and even taught younger kids when she was in school. Now, she has a degree in Special Education, is an Assistant Pastor, an author, and owns a book publishing company.

James, my second born, always loved to watch people and study their minds. He also loved to help people. I chuckle now when I think about how he always said he would be Batman when he grew up. Now, I look at him, and I can truly say he is a superhero. He is always helping others. He is a manager in retail and a psychology major.

Joanna has always loved doing hair. As a little girl, anything that was beauty or fashion related caught her attention. Now, she also works in retail as she develops her hairstyling skills. Her goal is to open her own hair salon one day, and I know she will do that and more.

My youngest, Jermeka, never missed a day teaching her dolls and teddy bears. Even though she is the youngest of the bunch, she has always acted like she is the mother hen. She hasn't changed a bit. You can always hear her giving her friends and others some wise advice. She is currently in school, majoring in psychology as well.

Though they all had different passions and desires, one thing is the same for all of them. They all love God and aren't ashamed to worship Him and serve His people. I am truly proud of each of my children, and they are my pride and joy.

I bet you are wondering, now why did she tell us all of that about her children? Well, first of all, I am a proud mother, and what proud mother doesn't like to share her children's successes? However, most importantly, I shared this with you to tell you about one of the most important lessons having children taught me: how to be tenacious about every dream and desire you have in your heart.

GODLY TENACITY

Being tenacious or having tenacity means being determined. After everything I experienced as a young adult, everything in me wanted to quit, throw in the towel, and give up on life. However, when I saw my children staring up at me every day, I knew I couldn't do that. I knew I had to press forward, be better, and do better. Not just for me, but for them. My biggest goal became making sure that my children had a life that was better than mine. I refused to allow anything to get in the way of that. Because I was tenacious, I achieved that goal, my children are doing amazing things in life, and I am now free to live my life as I please, knowing that I raised my children as best as possible.

I want you to take a moment and think about your biggest goal. What is it that you want or desire in your life? Maybe you don't have children or your own family yet. Perhaps your goal is to lose weight, write a book, start a business, go back to school, or get a promotion on your job. Whatever your goal is, I want to encourage you to go after it. Whenever we have a goal, dream, or desire, the enemy will do everything in his power to keep us from achieving it. Have you ever wondered why as soon as you make up your mind to do something, it seems like all hell breaks loose? This is because the enemy plans to make you give up.

No matter what the enemy throws your way, you must be determined to go after your dreams with all of your might. In the Bible, God never says that life will be easy, but He does promise to be with us every step of the way. I don't know about you, but knowing that God has my back gives me the power I need to accomplish everything He put in my heart to do.

Even as I worked hard to give my children the best life possible, things were difficult. My marriage faced challenges, and I will share those later. However, despite what I faced, I knew I couldn't give up. My children were counting on me. On the days where I felt like I didn't have the strength to go on, I prayed and asked God for help. He helped me every time. He is truly a present help in the time of trouble.

Do you know that people are looking to you and counting on you to achieve your goals? Yes! Some people are watching you every day. They are looking to you to see if they can make it too. This is why you cannot give up on your goals and dreams. You must do whatever it takes to see them through.

Let's be honest for a second. Sometimes, life can get hard. You can have a day where it seems like every way you turn, something goes wrong. On those days, it's okay to stop, take a break, breathe, pray, and get yourself together. However, no matter what you do, you cannot quit. Many times, when I went through hard times, I often asked God, "What's the point of all of this? Why is this necessary?" As I kept growing in God, I learned that trials and tribulations come to make us stronger. Many of us are very weak and don't have resilience because we keep giving up every time things get hard. Hard times build character, and if you don't allow them to build your character, you will be undeveloped. The worse thing you can do is try to make it to the top with poor character.

So, what am I saying to you? When hard times come, take a step back, but make sure you get back in the game. Don't give up on yourself, your dreams, your goals, or your aspirations. If you stay focused and keep pressing forward, you will accomplish your dreams. Whenever you think about giving up, stop, and think about how it will feel when you finally reach your goal! Think about how great you will look in the new dresses you have to buy because of your weight loss! Imagine yourself sitting at your book signing, celebrating the release of your new book. Can you imagine how great it will feel when you walk across that stage to accept your degree? What's on the other side of the difficulty you are facing will be so amazing, but to get to it, you must not give up.

Godly women are tenacious! We know that with God on our side, we cannot fail. We know that through God, all things are possible. We are daughters of the Most High King, and our Heavenly Father is backing us every step of the way! Make your Father proud. Make those who are watching your faith walk proud. Most importantly, make yourself proud.

I don't know what you are working towards or what you desire, but I want to leave you with this encouragement: You got it, girl! Don't throw in the towel. You are almost there! Let's Pray!

Lord,

Sometimes, life gets tough. It seems so easy to throw in the towel and walk away from what You have instructed us to do. Give us the strength to be tenacious. Help us to stay focused on our goals and dreams, no matter what comes our way. Give us the ability to endure everything the enemy throws our way. Give us the wisdom we need to maneuver around every obstacle that comes our way. Remind us that everything we do is for your glory. Remind us that everything we endure adds to the story and testimony we share to encourage others. We bless your name and thank you for every opportunity you give us to grow in character. In Jesus' Name we pray, Amen.

ACTIVITY THREE

Take a moment and think about one accomplishment you are proud of. What obstacles did you face as you worked toward that accomplishment? How did you press through despite the difficulties? Use the space provided to reflect on that accomplishment. Whenever you feel like giving up, open up this book, go to this activity, and remind yourself that you can do it!

TAKE 3!

In the space below, write your top three take-aways from this chapter.

But the Lord said to Samuel, "Do not look on his appearance or on the height of his stature, because I have rejected him. For the Lord sees not as man sees: man looks on the outward appearance, but the Lord looks on the heart."

1 Samuel 16:7 (ESV)

CHAPTER FOUR

THE HEART OF THE MATTER

M y second marriage was different from my first marriage in various ways. For starters, my second husband was 25 years older than me. Our age difference brought about challenges, but we worked through them. He was my friend, lover, provider, supporter, and the father of my youngest two children. He also took my two oldest children under his wing and cared for them as if they were his own. Our marriage was far from a bed of roses, but we made sure that we communicated about everything. When it came to the children, our methods may have been different, but we both desired to see them become their very best.

Around 2003, my husband became ill and had to leave his strenuous job as a log truck driver. It was great to have him at home more, however, I had to work more in order to make ends meet. It was difficult, but we made it work. On April 2, 2004, the children and I came home from work and school to find my husband, Joel, dressed and ready to go. He had been on a special diet due to his health issues, but on April 2, 2004, he demanded to have a burger. He wouldn't take no for an answer. The children and I thought it was strange, but of course, they didn't detest to having burgers instead of black-eyed peas and cornbread. We all got in the car and headed into town.

When we made it into town, we ran a few errands and went to the store. As we went around town, we encountered many of his friends. He spoke to everyone briefly but seemed to be in a bit of a rush to get to that burger he had to have. We went to Dairy Queen, ordered our food, and grabbed two tables. The children sat at one table, and he and I sat at another table alone. As we ate, he kept his arm wrapped around me and was extremely loving towards me. The children pointed at us and giggled. You see, my husband had never been an overly affectionate man, especially not in public, and definitely not in front of the children. That was probably the first time my children had ever seen us embrace each other in that way. What was also unique was that he allowed the children to have and do whatever they wanted. He was a very strict man, but other than fussing about having a burger, he didn't fuss about anything that day.

When we got home, I went next door to his sister's house to handle some paperwork for them, and as I did that, he burned the trash, took a shower, shaved his head, and got ready for bed. While I was next door, the children told me that he kept asking where I was and saying how late it was getting. At the time of his inquiry, it was still pretty early in the evening.

That night, we went to bed, and around 3:00 a.m., my husband started making weird grunting noises. I called the ambulance, but when they arrived, the Lord had already called him home. The rest of the night was a blur for me. I couldn't believe how a few hours changed my life forever. I felt so many different emotions. I was hurt and sad that I lost my lover and my friend, but afraid because I had also lost the father of my children, our protector, and provider. I couldn't believe that he had left me to raise four kids on my own. I'd dealt with death before, but nothing could be compared to this. It wasn't fair. I know I hadn't been the perfect wife, but I couldn't understand why God would take my husband away from me.

As it typically goes when you lose a loved one, everyone called, wrote, expressed their condolences, and told us they would be there if we ever needed anything. After we buried my husband, my four children and I got into the funeral home car and went home. We didn't stick around for the repast or anything. When we got home, reality hit me hard. I would have to spend the rest of my life without him.

Birthdays, holidays, celebrations, and even failures were difficult. There were times when I was disciplining or caring for the children, and I just wished he was there. But he wasn't. He would never be there again.

I was all mixed up in my mind. Some days, I would grieve my husband. On other days I would be angry with him for leaving. Then, there were days when I found myself jealous of my husband and God's relationship. The more I reflected on that last day we had with him, the more it seemed like he knew it would be his last day. In his actions, he said goodbye without it ever coming out of his mouth.

One day, I said to God, "Ya'll have just made a fool out of me! Both of ya'll knew this was going to happen, and neither of you said anything!" I felt betrayed by God and my husband. I thought to myself, "I was serving God and trying to be a good Christian woman, and He didn't even have the decency to tell me my husband was going to die. And my husband?

Here I was caring for you, and you didn't even prepare me for this day." For about three months after my husband's death, I didn't pray. When I did try to get on my knees to pray, the words wouldn't come. I would tell the Lord, "God, I have nothing to say to you."

My heart grew extremely hard and cold. To make matters worse, I felt all alone. No one came to sit and talk with me about grieving my husband. When I needed help and support, no one was there. It was as if people didn't know what to say, how to pray, or how to encourage me. They just watched me bury myself in my tears. I tried to find my way to heal and grieve, but I lost myself in the process. I would visit my husband's grave every day and talk to him as if he was there. I even took mail to the graveyard as if he could read it and tell me what to do.

It wasn't easy raising four children alone as a widow. Every day, I wondered when it would get easier, but it never did. It only got more manageable.

Even years after my husband's death, I didn't have a desire to move on and start dating. I honestly didn't trust men anymore. I felt that a man would just come into my life, love me, and then die on me. I even recall telling my children that if I started dating again, it would be for me, not for them. I didn't trust a man to come into their lives again. My heart was all messed up.

Throughout our lives, we will encounter situations and circumstances that hit us hard. In these moments, it will sometimes feel hard to breathe. If we don't manage these trials correctly, our hearts will grow hard and cold towards God. My husband's death was one of the hardest things I've ever had to deal with in my entire life. However, it taught me an important lesson about the posture of our hearts. When our hearts are broken, it's very difficult to move forward and see the beauty around us. Our hearts control everything we do, say, or pray about. This is why the Bible warns us in Proverbs 4:23 to protect/ guard our hearts. Everything flows from our hearts.

To protect our hearts, we must be aware of the things that can affect our hearts' posture. Often, we go through hard things and try to keep moving ahead in our lives without stopping to assess the damage that has been done to our hearts. Disappointments, break-ups, deaths, arguments, transitions, and even failure impact our hearts. When we go through moments like these, it is crucial to stop, breathe, and ask God to check our hearts.

My husband's death caused me to have some major trust issues, not just with people, but also with God. I had to pray and ask God to deal with those trust issues. If I had not allowed God to deal with the trust issues in my heart, it would have been difficult for me to accept the help God sent later in my life.

Take a moment and think about the difficulties you have faced in your lifetime. How did those challenges change your heart?

A lot of us are unaware of how our hearts have been impacted. As women, we are encouraged to be strong and keep doing for those around us. As a result, we are more prone to have years and years of pain stored in the corridors of our hearts. Who many may look at and call "a bitter woman" is actually a woman who has not had time to process the pain in her heart.

My sister, I don't know what you've experienced in your life, but I want to encourage you to allow God to heal your heart. He is not only able to, but He is willing. Psalm 34:18 says that God is close to the brokenhearted and saves the crushed in spirit. Even though it may feel as if God is far away and isn't concerned about you, this is not true. God cares. God knows. God wants to heal you.

The process of healing your heart will require you to surrender your pain, disappointment, frustration, and anger to God. Be honest with God in prayer. Don't try to say all the right words. Tell God how you feel and know that He can handle it. He understands. We don't serve a God who is not compassionate. He truly cares about our human condition.

Maybe you are reading this, and you feel like your heart is broken beyond repair. Maybe you feel like your heart has been out of commission for so long that you can't recover. Ezekiel 36:26 says, "And I will give you a new heart, and a new spirit I will put within you. And I will remove the heart of stone from your flesh and give you a heart of flesh." There is nothing too hard for God. He has the power to replace your broken and hardened heart with a new heart. Take your heart to Him and allow Him to do what He does best.

When I was dealing with my husband's grief, I didn't have a circle of Godly women to help me through it. Now, God has staffed my life with an amazing group of women who love, support, and pray for me. Additionally, even though my husband isn't here, God has sent amazing men into my life as well as my children's lives over the years. Even though we still miss Joel dearly and often wonder what life would be like if he were still here, we are at peace. If someone had told me that I would be in this place and that my heart would feel this whole, I wouldn't have believed them. However, my story is a true testament to God's healing power and His ability to renew the heart. Let's pray!

Our Heavenly Father,

We praise you for being the mender of hearts. Thank you for keeping us during storms and trials that we thought would kill us. We know that You have kept us alive for a reason. We also know that if we are going to become all that You said we could be, our hearts must be healed. At this moment, we lift our hearts to You. We ask that You would search our hearts completely. If there is anything unlike You lurking in our hearts, we ask that You remove it. God, we don't want the pain of our past to defer us from the beautiful things You have in our future, so heal our hearts, Lord. We thank You in advance for Your healing. We love You and praise You. In Jesus' Name we pray, Amen.

ACTIVITY FOUR

In prayer, ask God to reveal the things that may be lurking in your heart due to painful encounters. In the space provided, write the encounters and what it did to your heart. Do this for every difficult thing you have dealt with in your life. Next, pray over everything you wrote and allow God to minister to the broken areas in your heart.

TAKE 3!

In the space below, write your top three take-aways from this chapter.

Create in me a clean heart, O God, and renew a right spirit within me. Cast me not away from your presence, and take not your Holy Spirit from me. Restore to me the joy of your salvation, and uphold me with a willing spirit.

Psalm 51:10-12 (ESV)

CHAPTER FIVE

BE TRANSFORMED

After living in Catherine, AL for most of my life, in 2010, I moved to Huntsville, Alabama. My oldest children were already in Huntsville for college. I don't know what compelled me to move, but I knew it was time for a change for my youngest two children and me. I had no idea what would meet me when we arrived in Huntsville.

As I've said before, I have been in church my entire life. Growing up, my mother made sure that all of her children were in church every Sunday. Saturday afternoons were like Sunday school at our house. My parents divorced when I was around five years old, so I didn't spend a lot of time with my father until I became an adult. Like my mother, my father was a devout Christian. He loved the Lord and didn't mind telling anyone how good God had been to him. Even as an adult, Daddy would always remind me to pray and be kind to others. I can recall moments when I would take him to the doctor, and he would say to the nurses and those he encountered, "What the Lord say, ya'll? Tell me something good." He was looking for them to say something about God. If they didn't give him a reply, he would give them a scripture and encourage them to seek the Lord. The most valuable thing my parents could have ever taught me was to love God. Though I confessed Christ at an early age and got baptized, I was a fully grown adult when I really understood what it meant to walk with Christ.

When I moved to Huntsville, my daughters and I started attending a new church. It was here that I realized God moved me to Huntsville so that my relationship with Him could grow. Throughout my life, I'd experienced so much trial and tribulation. When I moved to Huntsville, I was in a place where I was tired! I was tired of the relationships that went nowhere. I was tired of the same mundane life. I was tired of the mess, gossip, drama, and living life my way. I wanted something new.

There were many times when I wanted to change and even prayed to God for change. However, the change didn't happen because I wanted to hold on to certain sins and even had the nerve to justify them. I was living a double life. I had one foot in God's will and the other foot in my desires. This didn't work with God. As the Bible tells us in Revelation 3:15-16, "I know your deeds, that you are neither cold nor hot. I wish you were either one or the other! So, because you are lukewarm—neither hot nor cold—I am about to spit you out of my mouth."

I had advice for everyone, but I wouldn't take any of my own. I was hurt, and I didn't want to relinquish the things I knew were wrong. Just as I did in my first marriage, I kept making decisions for my life based on what I wanted and not what God was instructing me to do. God moved me to Huntsville because the life I was living wasn't the life He had planned for me.

When my daughters and I started going to a new church, my relationship with God changed. I began to understand what God desired from me. I started talking to God more about everything, the good and the bad. The more I did this, the more our relationship grew. As our relationship grew, I noticed myself handing things over to God instead of fixing them myself. Each time I gave a situation over to Him, He worked it out for my good.

The more I drew closer to God, the more he began to clean my mind and heart. I began to end certain relationships, and I no longer desired to be apart of negative conversations. More importantly, my attitude began to adjust. I learned how to be patient and more compassionate to others. I stopped running to worldly things and actions to answer my problems and sought God for instruction and direction.

Whenever I sit back and think about the woman I used to be, I am astonished at how much God loves me. For so long, I didn't even know the relationship I have with God now was possible. If I did know it was possible, I certainly wouldn't have thought I was worthy of it. Looking at me, no one would ever believe that I used to pride myself on stealing another woman's man or husband. People wouldn't assume that I once made late midnight calls for sex. They don't know how I used to reach for a bottle of gin, MD2020, or a wine cooler to relax my mind. They don't have a clue that I was once the type of woman who would fight you or pull out a knife on you in seconds. God completely transformed my life, and I am grateful for it. What I thought was embarrassing is now my testimony. God delivered me and has shown me how He wants to use me to help others.

God loves us, even though we don't always love Him. His words are true; He will never leave us nor forsake us despite what we do or how far we drift away from Him. He knows what is best for us, and when we draw closer to Him and submit to His process, He gets the best out of us.

If you truly want your life to transform, you must

be serious about your relationship with God. You can't do it alone. You will wear yourself out trying to fix your life without God. He has the power to do the things we can't do. He can heal the places that have been broken for years. He can remove the people we are afraid to walk away from. He can reveal to us the things that have been hidden behind pain and turmoil. He can provide us the opportunity to start our lives over after we feel like we've messed everything up. Only God can do these things.

I don't know where you are in your relationship with God, but I want to encourage you to make it the most important relationship in your life. I know it may be fun to hang out with your friends and talk to everyone else, but a relationship with God is more vital than a relationship with anyone else. If you want to be married, make sure your relationship with God is healthy first. If you're going to be a millionaire, you need to be closer to God so that you will know what to do when you get those millions. You need God for everything you desire to do and become. Again, there is no way you can do it without Him.

Developing a stronger relationship with God will require you to be intentional about the time you spend with Him. Be sure to set aside uninterrupted time to pray and listen to God. Also, everything you need to know about God can be found in His word. Read the Bible daily, and challenge yourself to find new revelation about who God is. As you draw closer to God, know that things in your life will begin to shift and change. You may not be around the same people anymore. You may get a new job. You may even stop eating the same food, listening to the same music, or visiting the same places. Remember, when God comes into our lives, He transforms our lives for the better! Every change that happens in your life when you draw closer to God is for your good, so embrace it.

As you draw closer to God, the biggest transformation will be in you! When God gets done with you, don't be ashamed or afraid to tell people where you come from. Boast about the transformation God has made in you! Testify of His goodness so that others will be encouraged to seek Him. Let's pray!

God,

Thank You for sticking closer to us than any friend or family member ever could. We are so very grateful that You didn't leave us in our mess. Thank You for not allowing us to lose our lives in pursuit of sin. Thank You for giving us another opportunity to get things right with You. God, we desire You to come into every area of our lives. Transform us so that those we come in contact with will be transformed as well. Make us new in You. Change our hearts and our minds. Change how we view ourselves and oth-

ers. Do it all for Your glory. It's in Jesus' name we pray, Amen.

ACTIVITY FIVE

In the space provided, create a timeline of your relationship with Christ. When did you receive Christ? When did you really start to walk with Him? How has your relationship with God grown? Be sure to include the dates and events that made you draw closer to or pull away from God. Once you are done, give God a fresh yes. Recommit yourself to growing in your relationship with God.

WHAT?!

TAKE 3!

In the space below, write your top three take-aways from this chapter.

Not only that, but we rejoice in our sufferings, knowing that suffering produces endurance, and endurance produces character, and character produces hope, and hope does not put us to shame, because God's love has been poured into our hearts through the Holy Spirit who has been given to us.

Romans 5:3-5 (ESV)

CHAPTER SIX

ENDURE THE PRUNING

Right when I was starting to get the hang of my new life in Christ, I became ill. It didn't make sense. I asked God, "Why is it that right when I'm on my journey to freedom, You have allowed me to get sick? I'm trying to live according to Your word. Why are You punishing me?" I don't have any lies to tell you. I was so sick, I started to think God hated me or something. I went to doctors and specialists, but no one could tell me what was wrong with me. There were days when I was so sick, I couldn't eat or drink water. It was like everything I put in my body burned my stomach. Things got so bad that I was hospitalized. Some of the people who knew how ill

I was wondered if I was going to make it, except my church family and siblings in California. When they found out about my sickness, they instantly began to pray and intercede on my behalf. It's so important to have people who listen to the report of the Lord instead of man!

As my family and friends prayed over me, my faith was restored. I believed that my healing was complete, and I asked God to give me the strength to endure the process. I believed that I would live and not die. As my faith in my healing grew, I could hear God more clearly about what He was doing in me, and why He had allowed me to become ill. He told me that there were still somethings inside of me that needed to be healed. In the natural, my body was sick, but supernaturally, God was cleansing me. There were somethings inside of me that needed to die if I was truly going to become the woman God had designed me to be.

You see, I had released the old habits I used to do. Now that I had grown, it was time for God to prune the areas that would keep me from growing and producing fruit.

In prayer, God reminded me of my beloved plum tree. When we lived in Catherine, we had a huge plum tree in our front yard. That tree sat right in front of my bedroom windows. It was so big that its leaves and branches covered most of our side of the house. I loved that tree because of the extra privacy it allowed. As the seasons passed, my children and I would watch the tree. In the winter, we would notice how bare it was. In the spring, we would marvel at how the birds made their nests, laid eggs, and their children hatched in that tree. In the summer, we would enjoy the fruit the tree bore. The plums were so juicy and sweet that my children and I had to race to pick them up before the dogs got them!

One day, a storm hit our area. The plum tree was split into two parts. One part of the tree stood tall and strong, but the other part fell on our house. My husband worked long hours and had planned to take care of the tree, but never got around to it. One day, I decided to help him out, and the kids and I cut the tree up and removed the debris from our yard. As we were removing the tree, God instructed me not to just cut away the part that died but to also trim some of the branches that were unaffected by the storm. When my husband came home from work and saw what we had done, he was very proud and thanked us for doing it.

Well, our excitement was soon ruined by those who didn't think it was a good idea to trim the tree. People began to talk negatively about what we had done. They said, "Ya'll have killed that tree. It won't have no more plums on it." As the seasons went by, I started to think that maybe it wasn't a good idea to cut the tree. I worried that we had cut away too much and would never enjoy those delicious plums again.

One year later, I went out to look at the tree and noticed plum blossoms forming. By summer, there were so many plums on that tree, we couldn't eat them all fast enough. Even the dogs and the birds couldn't handle the overflow from the tree.

On my sickbed, God reminded me of this tree. He began to show me how much I had in common with that tree. You see, for so long, I lived a life that I enjoyed. I thought that everything I had was as best as it would get for me. Even though I was producing fruit, I had no idea that there was more in me. When the storms of life hit me, just like the tree, parts of me were damaged. Things were removed by choice and by force. Like that plum tree, I went through seasons where the dead parts of me were just hanging on to me. Even though they didn't serve a purpose, I held on to them. I was so busy wallowing in my brokenness that I didn't make time to allow God to step into my life and heal me. Once I did, God just didn't want to stop at removing the dead habits. He also wanted to prune me so that I could bear more fruit. After all those years of watching that tree, it wasn't until I was down that I realized how much that tree and I had in common.

Once I realized what God was doing in my life,

I began to heal. I healed from the depression, bitterness, heartbreak, anger, and disappointment that had been hidden in my heart for years. When I didn't have the energy to get up and be active, I prayed and allowed God to reveal things that were deep down in my heart. I released the regret of bad decisions that I'd made. I resolved the trust issues. I let God touch the bad memories that I'd held on to from my childhood.

When I finally got up from my sickbed, people said I looked so different. It wasn't just because of the natural weight I lost, but also the dead weight I lost in the spirit. I was a pruned woman, and I was ready for God to allow my fruit to testify of His goodness. Today, I am a walking witness of God's healing power. I can still get around. I'm in my right mind. My health isn't perfect, but I am taking the steps every day to improve my wellbeing. The memories of the process I had to go through will forever be with me to remind me of the goodness of the Lord.

As you've read my story, do you see where you may have a thing or two in common with that plum tree too? You see, sometimes, we will find ourselves in the middle of life's storms. Sometimes, these storms will cause us to lose things that we thought were important, things we thought we needed. Things can get so bad that we don't know left from right, or up from down. It's in these moments when we think we won't recover or gain back what we lost. Can I tell you something? That's the entire point of the storm! God doesn't want you to just recover. He wants you to acquire more than you ever had before.

Some of the things we lose in the midst of life's storms were just stuff and baggage, keeping us from being where God desires us to be. We have to look at this situation and recognize that God is pruning us of the things that keep us from becoming who He designed us to be. All of our storms look different. For some, the storm will come in the form of a lost job, death, forced relocation, or even the ending of relationships. Before you get upset or depressed, ask God to reveal to you the purpose of the storm. Allow Him to show you the good in every goodbye.

If God has you in a season where it seems like you are losing things that were once important, He may be trying to prune you. I encourage you today to start pruning your life. Get rid of things and people that are holding you back and pulling you in all directions. Break loose of the things that are choking your fruit and your ability to produce fruit. Stop being so corrupted by things that mean you no good.

When you embrace the pruning process, you can see God's face much clearer and hear His voice much louder. Then, you will be prepared to receive the blessings God wants to overflood your life with. The pruning process is sometimes painful and uncomfortable, but don't give up in the process. 1 Peter 5:10 says, "And after you have suffered a little while, the God of all grace, who has called you to his eternal glory in Christ, will himself restore, confirm, strengthen, and establish you." Endure the discomfort so that you can be blessed beyond measure with enough to share with others. Let's pray!

Father,

Your name is greater than any other name. We acknowledge You as the God who knows everything. We acknowledge You as the God who knows our end from our beginning. Nothing is hidden from You. You know everything and see everything. For this reason, we know that we can trust your plan for our lives. Lord, sometimes, the things You allow don't feel good, but Your word lets us know that all things work together for the good of them who love You and are called according to Your will. Give us the strength to endure the process of pruning. Give us the strength to let go of everything that is keeping us back. We desire to grow in Your will and purpose for our lives. Help us to realize and recognize the things that are holding us back. Help us even as we grieve the things You choose to take away from us. Give us peace in knowing that You won't just restore, but You will give us better than what we ever had. In Jesus' name we pray. Amen.

ACTIVITY SIX

Going through a storm of life isn't the only way God can prune us. Honestly, sometimes God will allow storms because this is the only way He can get our attention. Don't wait on a storm to begin removing unnecessary things and people from your life. Pray today and ask God to reveal everything in your life that keeps you from living a life that is pleasing to Him. As God reveals these things to you, write them below. Next to each thing you write, pray for wisdom on removing these things from your life. After you pray, write your plan to prune your life of everything holding you back from producing good fruit!

TAKE 3!

In the space below, write your top three take-aways from this chapter.

I lift up my eyes to the hills. From where does my help come? My help comes from the Lord, who made heaven and earth. He will not let your foot be moved; he who keeps you will not slumber. Behold, he who keeps Israel will neither slumber nor sleep. The Lord is your keeper; the Lord is your shade on your right hand. ...

Psalm 121:1-8 (ESV)

WORDS FROM THE AUTHOR

I want to thank each of you for supporting my very first book. The process of writing this book wasn't an easy one, but it was worth it. After you have read my story, my prayer is that you will be encouraged along your journey to possessing the wisdom, heart, attitude, and tenacity of a Godly woman. God has so much in store for you. It doesn't matter what you've gone through or what you've been through. As long as there is breath in your body, you have a chance and opportunity to turn your life around for good.

As you can see from reading my story, I haven't always been the woman I am today. I've done a lot of things I'm not proud of. I've broken a lot of innocent hearts. I've said things I can't take back. I've been in situations that should have killed me. I've experienced sickness, grief, loss, betrayal, and that's just the stuff I've placed in this book. However, despite everything that I've endured, I'm still here. Despite everything I've done, God still isn't done with me yet. He still has a purpose and a plan for my life. Nothing I've done or said can ruin that purpose.

I want to encourage you to chase after the life God has for you. I don't care what you have done or who you did it to; trust God to transform you. As God transforms you, be okay with the people who can't appreciate the transformed you. Just as those friends and associates walk away, God will send people into your life who will be able to support the new thing He is doing in your life.

Many times, when God has worked things out in our lives, we tend to look down on those who are still in the midst of their processes. Keep your heart pure and pray for those that God is still working on. We aren't better than anyone; we are just in a different place in our process. No matter how far you go, stay close to God. Continue to read His word, and not just to say you read it. Read it for understanding. The Word of God has the power to transform our thinking and how we live, but we must be open to it.

Everything that you have gone through is a part of your story and testimony to the world. Don't be ashamed of it. Use it to set others free.

If you ever feel like the world is against you and that no one understands, trust that God sees, hears, and knows what you are going through. When you feel alone and as if no one loves you or cares, know that God loves you more than you love yourself. Know that everything that concerns you, concerns Him. Trust His timing. He is going to turn things around for you as you submit to His process.

Finally, know that I am rooting for you and praying for you! Be sure to revisit your favorite chapter in this book whenever you are feeling down or off track. Take a moment and look at the assignments you completed, and remind yourself how far you've come. I am proud of you for completing this book, and I hope to read your story one day! With God on your side, not even the sky is the limit!

Praying for you always,

Doris W. Sanders

Giving thanks always and for everything to God the Father in the name of our Lord Jesus Christ;

Ephesians 5:20 (ESV)

ACKNOWLEDGMENTS

First and foremost, I want to thank my Lord and Savior, **Jesus Christ** for giving me words to encourage the world. To my mother, **Rebecca Burrell Shaw**, my father **John Jones**, and my stepfather **Earl Lee Shaw**: Thank you. I miss each of you dearly, but I know you are safe in the Father's Arms. Without each of you, I wouldn't be here. I am thankful for the wisdom and morals you all instilled in me. I am thankful for the love you provided me when you were here.

To my late husband, **Joel Sanders, Sr.** thank you for every year we shared. Thank you for being an amazing father to our children and the best husband to me up until your last breath. You taught me so much about life and myself. I will never forget you.

I want to give special thanks to my wonderful children. **Jessica**, thank you for believing in me and publishing my story for the world to read. I am forever grateful. To my son **James**, thanks for being there whenever I needed you. I am so grateful for how you always make sure I have any special meal or home appliances I want. I love you, son. **Joanna**, you were the first person I told that I was going to write a book. You said, "Go Ahead, Mama!" I am so thankful for your push and your support. Thank you for staying on top of me and always pushing me to write, even when I didn't want to hear it. Thank you for being my nurse whenever I was sick, and doing everything from feeding to bathing me. I will never be able to repay you for everything you did to make sure I was okay and comfortable. I love you. To my baby girl, **Jermeka**, you have been my rock from day one. You never hold anything back, and I'm so proud of you for always being confident enough to speak your mind. Your encouragement means the world to me. Thank you for always making sure your mama is straight and helping me as the little mother hen in our family. I love all four of you more than words can ever express. I am truly proud of the adults that you all have grown to be.

To my awesome and amazing grandson, **Chad II (Tank)**, my prayer partner, and my WWE Friday

Night Live date. You mean so much to me. Words cannot explain it. The day I found out that you were on the way into the world, my whole life changed. The love that you have brought into this family is simply remarkable. The first time I told you the name of my book, you never forgot it, and you are always the first to say the title. You never fall short of praying for me whenever I ask you to. One time, we were both sick. You had an ear infection, and your fever was high. But you got out of the bed, went down on your knees, and prayed for me. You said you didn't want your grandmama to be sick. I fell on my knees beside you and began to pray with you for both of us. Chad, I love you for molding your grandmama to be the world's greatest granny. Thank you for being such a light in my world.

Special thanks to my **Sistas with Purpose (SWP)!** **Lorie**, you have been nothing but the best. You have been my friend, counselor, big sister, prayer partner, and a shoulder to cry on. You took me under your wings and molded me spiritually, mentally, and physically. You gave me tough love and held me accountable for the things I needed to do. You taught me how to listen more and talk less; even when I think I am right, I am grateful that you always encourage me to be still and listen for God. You believed in me when you first met me. You didn't let me give up or run backward. I will forever be grateful to you.

Marvelene, you have been my friend, big sister, prayer partner, Bible study buddy, and my girly! Thank you for allowing me to exhale as I was taking this new journey of life. You prayed for me night and day. I know there were times that you wanted to tell me to shut up, but you always allow me to vent and get out whatever I need to share. Thank you for holding me accountable and making sure I have fun but stay saved! LOL! Thank you for never allowing me to make excuses. I am truly grateful for you.

Roni, the woman with all the wisdom, my big sister, friend, and prayer partner. Thank you for teaching me how to look at life in a whole new way. You taught me how to breathe and let go. Thank you for being so kind and always available when I need a shoulder or an ear.

Grace, my friend, thank you for keeping me grounded with words of prayer. When both of our families were facing difficulty in health, you were there to encourage me to keep the faith. Thank you for being there for me, even as you went through your trials. I am grateful that God placed us in each other's lives.

Ezralene, you are a woman of few words, but it is always powerful when you speak. Thank you for the laughs and for always giving me the space to be me!

To all of my **SWP sisters**, I love each of you. Thank you for taking me in, grooming me, loving me, covering me, and always being a safe space for me. I will never forget you all.

To my siblings, **Lathan, Clara, Jerry, Debra, and Christine,** thanks for being there for your baby sister. Thanks for protecting, loving, and spoiling me. I am here today because of your support. I will forever hold the beautiful memories of our childhood in my heart. I love you all.

To my siblings, **Arthur, Arnetta, Reddie, Maggie, Bessie, LeCardy, LeRoy, Johnnie Mae, Elnora, Bernice, Juliet, and Abraham**: Even though we didn't grow up together, you all accepted me and loved me. I am so grateful for all of the love, support, prayers, laughter, and great meals we've shared. To **Abraham, Bernice, Reddie, and Juliet,** I miss you all. I thank God for the time He allowed us to share. Though you are no longer here, the memories I have with you will forever live on in my heart.

To my sister-in-love, **Hattie**, I love you more than words could express. Thank you for opening up your home to my family and me whenever we visit California. The conversations we have shared will forever be engraved in my heart.

To my amazing pastor, **Pastor Adrian Davis**, I could write a whole new book about you and your kindness. Before I became a member of your church, you told me, "One day, you will be saying, 'I am a member of All Nations.'" I just smiled and said, "I don't know about that."

Now, look at me, a proud member of All Nations. Thank you so much for everything you have poured into me. Since being under your leadership, I have grown leaps and bounds, spiritually, emotionally, and mentally. Over three years ago, you first prayed for me concerning my feet, and I've not had pain in them since then. You are a true and proven man of God with a heart of gold. You never meet a stranger or anyone too messed up for you. I am forever grateful for how you took my daughter underneath your wings and molded her as if she were your own. What you didn't know was while you were molding her, God was preparing you to make an impact in the lives of her entire family. Thank you, Pastor AD. Words cannot express the love that I have for you. May every day bring you peace, love, and joy. To my entire **All Nations Worship Assembly- Huntsville family**, I love each of you with the love of Christ!

ABOUT THE AUTHOR

Doris Williams Sanders was born and raised in Catherine, Alabama. She is the proud mother of three daughters (Jessica, Joanna, and Jermeka) and one son (James). Doris also has one grandchild (Chad), whom she loves dearly. She is a graduate of Ashford University and currently resides in Huntsville, Alabama. Doris is a member of All Nations Worship Assembly- Huntsville, where she serves as the co-lead for Sistas with Purpose, a Women's Lifegroup. At ANWA-HSV, she also serves as an ordained Deliverance Minister.

Her greatest goal in life is to be a true, Proverbs 31:26 woman. Doris has a special gift to empower and support young, single, and married women, especially those who are widows and first-time moms. Doris looks forward to producing more books and resources for women. Her desire is to help women all over the world by the grace of God, the works of her hands, and the words of her testimony.

A MESSAGE TO THE WORLD

I want the world to know the pains and struggles that I had to endure; The things that made me stronger and whole in the Lord.

I want the world to know how I've been ridiculed and mistreated, only because I helped someone who felt my help wasn't worth anything.

I want the world to know how I've been knocked down by those who were supposed to love me!

I want the world to know how the enemy tried over and over to take my life. But, what he didn't realize was that it was only a test of my faith!

I want the world to know how I kept giving and giving, even though I never heard the words, "Thank You."

I want the world to know that when my time on earth has expired, I don't want anyone to share memories of my life filled with lies, regrets, guilt, and shame.

Don't place flowers on my grave or chose my favorite color to wear to my funeral, for I will be pure and white, resting in the arms of Jesus and covered in His red blood!

These are my words, spoken from my heart to the world. Don't try to duplicate them. Only the pain of my heart, the bruises on my hands and knees, the miles on my feet, and the teardrops from my eyes can tell my story! What will your story look like?

Doris W. Sanders

STAY CONNECTED

Thank you for reading, *WHAT?!*. Doris looks forward to connecting with you and keeping you updated on her next releases. Here are a few ways you can connect with the author.

INSTAGRAM @doriswsanders
FACEBOOK Doris Sanders
EMAIL   d.dorissanders@gmail.com
WEBSITE   www.doriswsanders.com